'I remember when the iron was new and strong and the woman was happy. I remember before the buildings burned.'

In Praise of *Neuro, Typical*:

"In 'Self-Portrait of Me Living Up To the Voices in My Head' the speaker imagines herself prismed through alternate, or 'quantum' versions of herself, a continuing meditation on viewing one's individual history as emotional plot points on a time line. *Neuro, Typical* does, indeed frame the speaker's history in relation to perceived calamity. 'Everything will be before and after the fire now.' I don't think anyone could say it better."

-Jonathan Travelstead
Author of *How We Bury Our Dead* and *Conflict Tours*

"Katie Darby Mullins writes poems that hike steadily into the unexpected—they do not leap or gambol, they sometimes dance and occasionally they sit, laughing, on their asses. 'This poem is a ball of yarn,' she writes, and perhaps that is the better metaphor: Mullins has spooled language around the pieces of herself, and she will unravel it for you, line by line, with precise grace and candor. You might forget, as the spool is laid out around you, that you are about to be confronted with a moment of naked, half-ashamed love."

-Charlie Ericson
Author

"In this breathtaking first collection from Katie Darby Mullins, she dives deep into the wreckage of illness, a housefire, and numerous relationships—both with others but also with herself—and swims to the surface bringing us these sometimes painful but always luminous poems. Fierce and personal, her voice brings us her hard-won wisdom, telling us that, '...what I know is that it still takes decades/ for a woman to disappear and come back:/ and it's harder still when no one knows/ she's missing.'"

-Rob Griffith
Author of *The Devil in the Milk* and *A Matinee in Plato's Cave*

Katie Darby Mullins

Neuro, Typical

Chemical Reactions & Trauma Bonds

Summer Camp Publishing

Summer Camp Publishing
PO Box 472
Banner Elk, NC 28604
SummerCampPublishing.com
Email: SummerCampPublishing@Gmail.com

Edited By: Ali Braenovich
Cover Art: Matthew Taylor Wilson
        MatthewTaylorWilson.com
Interior Design: Brooks Rexroat for Summer Camp
Publishing

First Edition
Isbn: 978-1-7353637-0-7
Printed in the United States of America

NEURO, TYPICAL
Chemical Reactions & Trauma Bonds

For Andy, Grace, & Charlie

Regret, or An Apology

No lightning struck when
> The house caught fire
Or when a stroke ricocheted
> Through my brain stem
Cutting this body in half
> With ragged scissors,
One side feeling nothing,
> The other, on fire.

Nail this thesis to your church door:
> I have kept my pain
Secret for so long,
> I always knew there was something
Wrong with me. Driving,
> I might absentmindedly think
"I could have a heart attack now
> Or now, or now, or now...."
Until I got home. You can medicate
> Fears like the house catching fire:
Hook up cameras so you don't
> Have to keep driving to check,
But this, the stroke: I knew
> The storm was coming
And I held my breath. I waited
> Like I've been under water for years.
The secret now isn't the pain.
> People can look back and see

I fought, I worked so hard to wake
    Up some days and they understand.
I have a new secret: I am relieved
    And when I tell people they think
I am sick and depressed. But I was always
    Sick and depressed: now I'm not waiting
For the disaster I've known was coming.
    You say "self-fulfilling prophecy" one more time
And I swear, a plague of locusts
    Will swarm from my mouth,
Wrap around and protect me
    Because the plagues aren't meant
Against me anymore. They prop
    Me up, make me more powerful.

Do not mistake my weakness for weakness:
    I am a wolf in a sick dog's body,
Dizzy but still a predator, never
    Fully ready to give up the hunt.

I'm sorry. You asked how I was
    And for 31 years I said "fine"
When the truth was my earthly body
    Was melting inside itself
With a strange disorder. Betrayal
    In the wires, my own DNA the Judas,
Not totally culpable, but necessary
    For any salvation narrative.

Have I been saved, you ask?
>I am alive. I'm sorry I can't say more,
Because sometimes I want to scream
>In exquisite joy over something
As simple as iridescent butterflies
>Or I want to cry when I am happy
Because I can finally translate
>An easy Spanish phrase again
He olvidado tanto, y todavia—
>No one understands why a slice
Of what used to be comes back
>And for a second I feel new and old
And like I am old brain and new brain
>Slammed together in the same

Strange body. Maybe the old me
>Occupies the blank space,
The unfeeling corridors of the right
>Side of my body.
I promised an apology. Some regret.
>I'm sorry I regret nothing.
I do not like this new slow model,
>But I feel a plague coming on
And while old cocoon clearly forgot
>To paint the door with goat's blood
But that is all the new animal never forgets—
>Protection is its own neuroses.
I am sorry. I have thrown away my bucket

Of goat's blood, made peace
With never having life inside me
And I will become the thunderstorm
Of hail and fire, because this storm
Has been a long time coming,
And I have always been someone
Drawn to flame, even as I am raining down
And still—no lightning. Next time.
No regret, except the lie I held, *I'm fine*.
No lo siento. Even though everything
In me knows that I should be.

In Preparation for Heartbreak

Carry this message in your bones,
Made of holes: not aerodynamic, like
Birds—hard and cold, heavy chainlink.
The first time you realize that everyone
Dies, even you, you die your first death—
Since before, there were a hundred
Ways to waste a lazy day, not
Knowing of its loss. You die again

When you learn what *forever* means,
Again when someone uses knowledge
Like that against you—they said *forever*.
And this is your fault anyway, who believes
A fairy tale? Or just one definition? Maybe

The only *forever* you trust is death,
But you are allowed small ones in life:
You'd think knowing how short forever
Is, you'd take fewer naps or smoke less
Or take up running, write letters, read more
But you say defiantly (in front of people),
With a lighter, "Gotta go somehow, right?"
        Who knows what you'd say in the dark.

Katie Darby Mullins

Reasons I Can't
Let Her Call Me "Mom"

One spring I helped raise opossums,
Thrown out of the pouch they were connected
To by their mother's nipples when she
Was hit by a car. They were embryos,
Paper-thin skin, you could see the milk-filled tube
Slide down their throats and into their stomachs.
The little girl, no longer than my index
Finger, learned to bite first, and was already
Growing her own pouch. Created from the womb
To create. If she could speak English,
She couldn't call me "mom" either.

Caterpillars turn into butterflies, sure, but how—
The wings already tucked inside their spongy, leggy
Tube-bodies. Even when they are small,
transformation built into their every cell
No matter what someone does to help
Them survive along the way. They grow,
Rage, and then lock away, I presume with
Headphones and a Tori Amos record
                (like I did)
And they turn themselves inside out. After,
They walk around this world with their guts
Flying them around. They don't need a mother.

Raccoons have to be bottle fed. Most babies
Need tube feeding, but a raccoon grabs you
With its tiny fingers like an infant. They want
To flip upside down and lay on their back
But you have to keep their heads upright,
To make sure they don't breathe in nutrition
They're supposed to ingest. Sometimes my eyes
Fill with tears because I love the raccoons
And I know that we're preparing them to be wild.
Sometimes my eyes fill with tears because for a second
I imagine that this is my baby, my stepdaughter,
And I am going back in time, and we are bonded
Physically now like we are in my heart, and here
The raccoons can call me "mom" and I can feel it
And no one gets their feelings hurt. I cannot stop
Rocking them, I cannot stop, even though
The fur already smells like forest, different
And foreign, and still not for me.

Define Your Terms

"There are no good or bad people"
-Charlie, who is frustrating to define

My therapist says (I hate
To start conversations this way)
I need "a word for Charlie" —
Maybe then I'll understand. She says
Come up with a word: but what word
Means "I wish I was your mother?"
Am I a bad person to want that?
                                    Like always,
I've withheld enough information
To protect myself from a doctor: she
Knows you helped post-stroke,
You were a student, now are some
Other animal, but she has no idea
She shares your mother's name.

                        *

If there are no bad people— worse,
No bad acts, just humans moving
Through the world, every choice
Creating good and bad outcomes—
It's 4 AM and Kenyon College is in my head,
Default-setting, default-setting...

…What the hell is water?
Natural, hard-wired, default-
Setting, which is to be deeply
And literally self-centered—[1]

Then there are no good people,
Either. You know. We fought,
You won. But—
You say I'm a good person.
So why would I want to take
You from your family—
That's not it. You came from them.
They are *need.* I am *want.* But that's
Not how I meant it, at all. I want all
Of us, but— *Self-centered. Hard-wired.*

*

I wish, I wish, I wish, I wish

*

---

1. In honor of David Foster Wallace, you should always footnote DFW. The author listens to this address at Kenyon College some nights when she can't sleep. It almost never works. She's always willing to try again.

There is a moment last November where, on an airplane, we both squeezed as tightly into our seats as possible so we didn't touch. But after your head, bobbing like a lure, finally gave up and found sleep on my shoulder, I let you stay there. I needed you to so I could lie to myself. Lying is wrong but waking you up would have hurt me: I don't know what people expect of me. I am not perfect. I knew I would never get that lie again.

*

I am an adult.
I do not *believe* in wishing.

*

<u>Things I Feel Guilty For</u>

- Having a stroke
- Being sick
- That being part of your story
- The time you saw my shoulder fall out of socket
- The time you caught me standing on our desk, cane and all *((maybe doing that at all))*

- Fighting you so hard when you tried to help that I made you say *Why don't you let people who love you take care of you* with a voice so desperate I hadn't ever heard it from you *((*note: can't ever make you sound like that again))*
- Needing you, the whole time, even when I said I didn't
- Saying "Thank you," and you coiled (re-coiled?) and said, "Please, don't say that, don't just act like you're OK with this." *(thank you for this gift— jackass)*
- Finally letting you help, making you relocate the other shoulder when it fell out of socket
- *How can I protect you from me?* I can't protect myself or I wouldn't need this list
- So much—all of this, over and over

*

When the doctor rattled symptoms
Like the pill bottle pharmacy
I will have on my nightstand
For the rest of my life, jangling
And spilling and so much noise,
One thing I caught was "will die
If you become pregnant"—
And I said, "I have a perfect kid, Grace"

That was before this, whatever you are.
My therapist, the one with your mom's
Name, really wants me to come up
With just one word for you. Friends?
I can't be your mentor: you surpassed
Me. I can't be your mom. It would
Literally kill me to be pregnant.
Plus, you're not a child, not a baby
And I can't spiral back through time
And learn you in those stages. And—
You have a mother. Her name is my therapist's.

Sometimes there are no words

The therapist says "empty nest." She says:
    "You are only 33 and Grace is going
        Into high school and you've had a stroke
        And your husband sick
            Everyone sick, the house on fire—"
But I didn't call a therapist
When any of those things happened
I did when I knew you were moving.
How do you push a baby bird

Out of their nest if they never
Lived with you?
And they aren't
Babies anymore. They're birds.
Maybe that's the word she's looking
For. Maybe we are birds.
That would explain the confusion.

*

Birds deal with each others' babies
As nature compels them: eating their eggs
Or laying their offspring in the nest
Of a tougher bird in hopes they'll make
It out, strong enough to live in Not Their Family.

Blue jays steal other birds' eggs
But they eat them. I am worse:
The "victim" of a nest-stealing cuckoo,
I'm the bird that sees something
That is Not Mine and I teach them
How to be mine.
            I am not a good bird.
            Maybe there are no good birds.

*

You like raising other people's children, one voice says.
Another, *you don't—can't—know what it means to be a
mother,* and that's true. I want to shove feathers down
my throat until it bleeds, the eggs already useless, my
womb full of a million tiny tufts, now as much of a
waste of space as it actually is. For years I felt invisi-
ble: but then, I could justify being the throw pillow, no
one notices what the
       feathers used to be, now nothing but space—
maybe—that's the word. Never mind. We're birds.

*

You worry you can't feel anything but I know secrets.
The truth about you is that your heart is so big that it
can't
Help but have picked up shrapnel along the way. You
Force yourself to feel? Believe what you need, but you
Force yourself numb. You have the weight of every
choice
You ever made piercing the muscle with glass shards
And you are not slow, you move
Too quickly and get too bored not to make a few
Judgement calls and you deserve so much better
Than I can give you because I am not a good person

And I want you to have a good person.
I needed you, sure, but now? I just like you,
Today it feels more important than need. Your eyes
get excited
When everyone else has forgotten how to even fake
Enjoyment. You watch people like they watch their
phones.
       You know I don't need to meet for coffee.
       You have real friends. I steal their time.
I do not want to add to the war zone in your chest,
The thrumming in your head, the buzzing
That I wish my own body didn't carry muscle memory
Of, that I didn't see and think

not him not him just make me do it again, no more fires no more
glass no bullets no fights no more self-hatred no more—just
give him a quiet I don't know, but learned to fake

don't you learn to fake it
stay excited and don't pretend that you know quiet
it won't make them love you more

it didn't make anyone love me more // sometimes I can feel my-
self disappear slowly, like a song on the radio crossfading into
dead air and static// yesterday I told someone I didn't exist in
my own life, just through other people's—they didn't hear me—

15

Katie Darby Mullins

*

Once upon a time, the knock
At the door wasn't a bill collector—
It was 9 AM and you were leaving
To be with your family for Easter
But you brought donuts, flavors scrawled
In the thin-sharp-black of your normal pen.
You looked shy. Maybe you saw through me
When I said it was OK that this
Was my first Easter without Grace.
Maybe you just wanted donuts and know
I will always eat the extra donuts
And maybe even now I am giving an out,
A way for your sincerity to be pocketed.
But you said, "Happy Easter, I'm sorry
I can't stay," and I realized maybe you don't
Have a word for this either. Maybe—
Maybe I just taught you to mimic—
You, a nest-stealing cuckoo's egg
In my blue jay nest where I consume
Other lives without realizing it,
          If there is no good or bad, does it matter
          If I know you aren't mine and want you
          Anyway, to teach you how to take
          The shattered glass out of your heart,

16

How to get the striated pieces
Of muscle out of your teeth and comfort
you when—

*

My kid once called us *feral*
And I think you might outgrow it,
But I am wild, moving on instinct to care
Instead of thinking it through.

The therapist who shares your mom's name
Says it's OK to love someone. I don't
Know if she understands what a wolf
Does in the dark to protect its pack.

Know this: you should leave. Be what
You were born to be, crack open trauma
And try to figure out which world
Is yours to emerge in.

*I'll stay at the perimeter. I'll watch what lurks. I won't have a
name for this. I will not care. A wolf doesn't need words. I will
stay in our dark while you move into the light and I will flash
murder teeth full of death and other muscle and—but we were
birds—*

You are always a mixed metaphor—
Someone who gives freely but can't
See that as empathy. And so am I:
Someone who pretends that she's a bird
When she's always a wolf, that she forgot
Desire and longing a long time ago,
That self-erasure is good:
>   But if there is no good or bad
>   Then I create a world where
>   We don't need a word, *default-setting*-nurture,
>   And you accept love, no questions,
>   And I don't negate, but add to family,
>
>   Because in my new cosmology,
>   You love yourself the way I love you
>   And I can borrow your eyes to see
>   Why I seem so damned important to you.
>   *But if I'm not?* Maybe only you change.

*

A wolf skulks, a wolf is skinny lean anger, a wolf knows noth-
ing of worth or worthlessness, a wolf would just protect you,
protect my stepdaughter, protect my husband, defend, defend, no
questions asked about how you became pack. A wolf picks up
pups and changes their directions. A wolf would just look at you
and think, "You are one of mine."

I am so jealous of the wolf.

*

Last thing: my office is full of my books because of you.
They are moving me next year because people
Are worried no one will see me when you leave—
>   I know this is too much sincerity
>   And you're red-faced, rubbing
>   An old shoulder injury where it
>   *Spiderwebbed* to quote you. But—
Maybe here is the harm in this poem:
Knowing you are embarrassed and still
Saying it: thank you for being my witness.
>   For years. And I will never see
>   My bookcase without thinking
>   Of your kindness, blonde curls
>   Lit up gold in sunlight—

A person who let me be maternal sometimes
When I needed that so much, who reminded me
How to think post-stroke. You deserve freedom—
                  Be unbound.
I'll keep watch of the dark, the one we know.
You keep my housekey, the few gifts you accepted,
The books. Keep the part of my heart I gave you—
On purpose—the one you've carried carefully for years.
The part that makes me think, maybe, the best
Any person can do, the closest to being a good person,
Is to carry and protect the hearts they've been given
In their guts, ready to fight with love, and ignore
Instinct to put them in their mouths, bite hard: gentle,
Even knowing they could coat their tongues with new blood.

I Open My Eyes to Make the Pictures Disappear

Sometimes I have other people's nightmares
A hand on my shoulder, blocks stacked
High on my chest, so I can feel each fractured
Rib finally give way. Angled faces flicker
And disappear like phosphenes, hushed breath
Crumples like paper bags and I know this story
Because I've lived it in a hundred alleys, a hundred times
Every time I cross a threshold to a dark world. The
nightmare is real even when it doesn't happen
                           (hasn't happened yet).

Second Person
(With Ehler's-Danlos Syndrome)

> *Ehlers-Danlos Syndrome is a disorder that affects the connective tissues in the body, which, in the author, causes hypermobility at every joint and contributed to a stroke she had in January 2017.*

How old was I when I became *you*
When my body/broken learned
How to slide pieces together
While the brain—me?—

Made sure no one noticed? "Your
Memory is not my memory,"
My friends say, my family. Of course.
I didn't want you to know. In fact, I was

You—thoughts carried around
In a cracked vessel, becoming kintsugi[2]
Seeing the space and lack under X-ray,
Tissue now gold between bone on bone.

Can I ever be the second person?
The one who says *yes, it hurts*
Always, always. Everything. Because
I hate her. I like the first, where I

Control the things I cannot fix:
I reset bone, I pop back in, I snap

2. The Japanese art of repairing broken pottery by filling cracks with gold; also an excellent Death Cab album.

Tiny joints from *dis-* to *located*.
The person who can hide a sling

From almost anyone, who covers
Any private injury like it is a treasure,
A secret. *You saw that?* It's an inside
Joke, now. My arm fell out of socket.

The snap? It doesn't hurt. I stopped
Crying out of pain when I was a kid.
Be strong, I say to *you*. *Don't cry
In front of anyone, for any reason.*

I hear it a hundred times: *You are weak,
You cannot possibly think anyone
Would believe you.* But I know the truth:
People have seen it happen. *Your—*

No, *my* body. People have seen me reset
My wrist. People watch ankles skate out
Crooked under legs. The crack of broken fingers
Turning steering wheels. I cannot keep

Promising myself I'll argue with the voice.
The voice is so sure. *You just want attention,*
A doctor said a long time ago. Now I say it to myself.
That was when the first person started disappearing.

You, Me, and All That Stuff We're So Scared Of

After Bruce Springsteen's "Tunnel of Love"

Do you want to hear the origin story
Or do you want to wait and let
It actually get interesting? The tunnel
Of love looks different for every

Couple on the ride, but sometimes
I wonder if ours took a detour:
Was the stroke always part of the tour?
Chronic illness? The fire? The Boss

Always made it sound like love itself
Was the scary part: being vulnerable,
Hoping the other person is as in love
As you are. No. That's not vulnerable.

I wonder if the man met a woman, fell
In love, and then she tore her shoulder out
(Like I always do, my Sisyphus[3] story:
This was always going to happen)— did

He stay when she couldn't think? Couldn't
Wash her own hair? A friend once said
We ask ourselves the wrong question
When we fall in love: we ask if we

3. A trickster who cheated death and angered the gods, Sisyphus is sentenced to rolling a boulder up a hill in Hades—and his shoulder probably hurts, too.

Love the other person unconditionally,
And "of course, of course." It's easy
To love sacrificially when the other
Person needs you. But the thing I was scared

Of? Wound up being that I *need* so much.
My friend says the real question is, "Would
I let this person take care of me?" Maybe
No one sitting in a bar, hoping to find love

Needs to think about this. It might never
Be part of their ride. But ours was haunted
And I can honestly say, a decade in, there's
Only two of us in this bed: what else,

After all this, could we possibly be scared of?

Katie Darby Mullins

Self-Portrait of Me Living Up To the Voice in My Head

I live many lives—
        In the version my head tells,

I use one to become
        A successful actress,

Break their hearts, hair
        Always tousled on billboards.

The voice doesn't care
        About my stage fright.

It wants me to tell some truth
        By lying professionally.

In one life, I am the professor
        And writer I am, but so much better.

You cannot stop the plagues
        Once God has begun vengeance

And in that life, I am
        Locusts consuming everything,

Animals raining. You cannot
        Stop me in that life.

In one: I am a perfect wife
        And mom. I am PTA

I am lunchtime visits, I am
        Make sure she's had something to eat

I take in strays. The voice likes
        Strays because that allows

Me to be gentle with someone,
        Allows me to be hard on myself.

In one I am a painter but the lines
        Are blurry and I don't know what I've done.

The voice doesn't love
        The painter. It whispers,

"That is more of a failure
        Than poet, truly"

And now we are both screaming
        Shut up shut up shut up

I wonder why the voice only
        Tells me of artists and family:

These things are never done.
        This poem is a ball of yarn

27

Tied so tightly around my neck
        And the voice pulls tighter.

In every life, the voice makes sure
        My existence is subjective

And no feather on a scale
        Will help me see the true measure,

Soul weight. Sometimes when I fall
        We watch the blood or bruise bloom

And I don't know how to say
        I did this for you—for us.

Like a weighted blanket, the voice
        Is a comforting albatross, an old friend.

I cannot tell you what my self portrait
        Of the woman the voice thinks I should be

Because every time I grasp a bar
        With sweaty fingers,

Barely holding, a new bar appears:
        And I'll reach it or drop, not knowing
        either self.

Why Male Birds Have Such Bright Feathers

"If you love enough, you'll lie a lot"
                    -Tori Amos, "Jackie's Strength"

How many women do I know who, after
marriage, live like caterpillars again, sucking
their brilliant hued (paper thin) wings back
into their guts, grown backward, walking around
like they were never meant to be anything else.
I keep seeing it: girls on the cusp of blossom,
just starting to show that iridescent sheen,
and then, as if that shimmery purple will outshine
the partner—it disappears.
                              Perhaps male robins
are so beautiful, so vivid, so the female
can see a reflection of who they would be
if they'd never met, if she weren't stuck
on the nest while he, red-breast plump,
goes out to make something of himself.
Perhaps beauty means more in the mirror.
But what I know is that it takes decades
for a woman to disappear and come back:
and it's harder still when no one knows
she's missing.

Katie Darby Mullins

To the Song I Was Afraid
I'd Wind Up Living In

> "I go home, take off clothes, smoke a bowl,
> watch a whole TV movie—I was supposed to
> be writing the most beautiful poems, and
> completely revealing divine mysteries up
> close—I can't say that I'm feeling all that
> much at all at 27 years old..."
>   -*Will Sheff (Okkervil River) "On Tour with Zykos"*

The record skips—or no, that spot, dried Coke
That spilled on CDs jammed into the spaces
I left them, naked. This one works, maybe
Too well: I'm 21 and terrified

My life is folding out like liner notes, dark
And drawn—they tell me what it means to be
A writer. (I hated meta-poems then—
Still do—and this is no exception.)

At 21, I felt so deeply that words
Echoed in my head like migraines, like buck
Shot, unnatural pain. I was only
Then learning "numb" is worse than "hurt," that days

A man yelled at me (I yelled back, loud)
Were easy when nights later, he would crawl

Across the console while sober, I drove.
He would knock over a long-flat drink,

And cry, but I'll keep his secrets. He meant
To say (I want to think) that pain is small
And numb is an ocean and I am the undertow
That brief glimpses of "truth" are fewer and fewer

That blank verse will fall apart so often,
And blankness is why: and now, a poem
About a poem. For people who write poems.
I heard that six-year clock ticking in Sheff's

Soft voice, the breaking in the word "whole,"
As two syllables (please read it that way here).
I was supposed (one beat) *to be writing poems*
I would think, sometimes with the television

On, yelling back, so loud. Now, more than ten
Years passed, I know: there are worse things than not
Knowing *divine mysteries* (two beats) *up close*
And maybe I won't ever learn something

New (true?). But I can say that numb is not
The devil I feared it'd be: it's feeling,
What I was scared to lose, that seems so hard
When your (my) husband has surgery again,

In ICU, when you (I) know one word—
Stroke— when your (my) kid aches because
She doesn't understand how girls can be
Mean, even if you (she) is nice to them.

My life in parentheticals: it's hard
To put the pain in first person, to call
The truth out loud, to curl like a comma
Around the driver (now, me in both roles)—

No. Put it all in second person. Try
To hold your breath when you smell hospitals
And don't flinch when you learn a new skill:
How to joke about your house on fire, smoke

Rising. Are you confused? You screwed up
The timeline. You learned that lesson at 25.
The sick was later. The girl cried later.
Did your heartbreak count less when you couldn't

Write a poem? When someone would say, "You should
Write about that?" And you hated them, small
Hate, because you felt it was a blow-off,
A way to get away from scary things,

Things you couldn't avoid. I love this new
Distance: I love my second person life
Where I keep my love to the corners
Of my heart and you (*you*) deal with the hard

Parts. (So many spondees: there's so much stress.)
But let me put *my* mind to rest—you will
Watch so many whole TV movies. You
Will enjoy them, you will laugh and cry. And—

I won't spoil the ending, but if you can
Allow yourself to write (*this again*) when
You feel like writing, it doesn't have to
Be divine. It doesn't. It doesn't.

I am not ready to listen, still. But
Maybe at 50 or 60, I will
Forget to feel so much, slough off the guilt
When I grab the remote. When I don't know

Where to end. When my biggest fear becomes
Not the numbness, but the glorious, white
Hot feeling of everything, the thrumming
    Of anxious wailing bombs in the distance.

Animal Stress

For Redbird at Mesker Park Zoo

Molted and balding, Redbird sits on a perch—
he's small for a Macaw. The feathers he has left
are thin and oily, clinging to his chapped skin.
His mate is gone. Since she'd been sent
to another zoo, he preened himself, plucked away
the parts of him she'd seen and loved. His colors,

once brilliant, dulled with age and constant
attention. I look at him, my jagged fingernails
shoved in my pockets, and I wonder if he is cold
without his feathers. The sign in front of his cage
promises that he doesn't hurt himself anymore,
but the follicles were damaged. His plumes will never
grow back. And in that way, I imagine he doesn't

have to hurt himself anymore: he lives that moment,
the loss, the pulling, over and over. His love's
absence is so much a part of him that he still sits
over to one side on the perch, waiting for her ghost.
I wonder now, lid permanently drooped from stroke,
what exactly I am waiting for when I look at a mirror.

To Those Who Left: You Dodged a Bullet

Pain will get easier
Motivating factor
Shoulder/wheelchair/brace
Blur of Velcro/plastic
Doctor to doctor to doctor
And a hundred explanations
Death rattle pill bottles
Arms length, knocked over
In what sleep I'm allowed
Words clipped/no energy
I was a bullet, fast
Straight and focused, but
Forgot: *I forgot everything*
Smoke and ash, explosion
At barrels/brainstorms
I—I am the bullet
They all dodged/ the shrapnel
Hide/lie down/clock pills
Lie. I'll say I'm fine.
It's all fine, it's a joke.
Bone on bone/marionette
Even strings can't hold me now
Count each crooked joint
And wonder who else counts

Who else looks down the days
Like packing muskets/am I there
In the future? Do I explode
Immediately or hit target first?
Should I laugh when someone
Has a memory (I know my husband
Suffers) they don't hold my breath
When it still hurts/it hurt/it hurts/it will hurt
I let hurt wake me up. What else
If not pain? I honor my weakness, my
Sacrificial friends/ get out of bed
Go as long as I can before
I tear apart the target. I will lie
Let other people tell the story
That my body was always fine.
That *she was so strong*, that—
What was that Vonnegut
Quote?—*Everything*
Was beautiful and nothing hurt.

I'm Finally Writing About the Fire, OK?

For years, all I could get on paper was "There was a fire"
but that wasn't true. Yes, there was a fire. Yes,
we had to leave the house—two months after
we married,
one month before our first Christmas. But that wasn't
the whole story, not by a longshot. That was just
the smoke. That was just the warning shot. That was just
the beginning of a pile of insurance paperwork
(I wanted to burn it: is that normal?) and explaining
we are all fine, yes, it's a miracle, yes, we got the dog.

A damned miracle. What was a miracle is I was high—
my wisdom teeth had been removed less than an hour before.
There's some irony. The wisdom of loss replacing
the wisdom of teeth, all through a Vicodin smokescreen.
And that's not all we had to laugh about: I couldn't hear
"We Didn't Start the Fire" for years without laughing.
I even had our whole story worked out to the cadence—
"Fire-men. On the roof. And they all had pickaxes!"
A miracle. Yes, they were able to save some of our things.

Because that's what we wanted. Things. Boxes full of trash
that we'd grown completely disconnected from. What I said
when we got out of the house? I looked at my husband
and said, you know, *everything will be before and after the fire now.*
Of course I was right. I was too young to know,
though, everything
is a point on a timeline. Do I sound angry? I
shouldn't. We were fine.
It was a miracle. And I mean that, it was. It could
have been worse.

Living in a hotel isn't what you'd think, at least, it
wasn't
all Keith Moon and room service and luxury. But on
Christmas Eve
we got Grace to bed and then poured Bailey's
into generic, Residence Inn coffee cups. We settled in
to watch
It's a Wonderful Life and the real miracle was there was no
irony. None. We sat silent and I wondered if I'd married
George Bailey and I was so happy in that moment, I
could have burst into flames, engulfed with my own
joy. Is that too heavy handed?

Every metaphor is a fire metaphor. I've earned that.
That's the good story. That's the moment I knew it was fine,
that our union was forged in strong heat, that we were welded
together. So why did I spend New Year's in bed, listening
to Steven Page sing, "The Old Apartment," crying every time
he screamed, "This is where we used to live/ I want them back?"
Because the fire narrative is not straightforward. Because the fire
does not make sense, even though that would be easier for everyone.
But we were fine. *Really*. It was a miracle, actually—

we made it out with no scars. Nothing anyone can see.
No one knows I was in a fire unless I tell them, which
I do. I want people to know that when there is smoke,
I emerge, and I am fine, and it is a miracle. But it is
five years later, five long years, and I still worry every
single day that I will come home and the house will
be gone.

What if we don't get the dogs? What if this time,
we don't get a miracle? I know that makes me sound
crazy.
The truth is, I always smell smoke now—ever since
that day,
high post-surgery, there has always been the scent of
ashes
in my brain. It's a miracle. We made it out. We're
fine.

Is that how I'm supposed to write about the fire?
After *miracle*,
"You should write about this," is the most common
comment
I got. Does this suffice? Does this explain it? And even
now—
I hope you still don't get it. Someone at Grace's
school
heard what happened and, wide-eyed, told me "Satan
must be terrified of you." I feel like you should know
that is part of the fire. Satan. But he's scared.
So am I. Still. It's a miracle.

What I Think About When You Say You Aren't Afraid of Anything

       —the night you tried to pull
a splinter from my finger with warm, old
tweezers—when you saw the blood,
and I winced. You apologized, but
Sorry sounded so foreign, like a stand-in
for what you meant, *I never wanted to
hurt you, I am so sorry pain is our language.*
I translate your body language, always have,
and I prayed that night I missed a subtlety,
that when I thought you said *stuck*, you'd said
This is normal, you are fine, this is fine.

I made you stop, leaving the splinter
inside my finger to fall apart on its own,
like a good-luck bracelet sewn by a Voodoo queen—
we laid, back to back, uneasy. In my nightclothes
I stepped out of the room, turning back
only long enough to see that your eyes were open,
that you wanted to say *Where are you going?*,
and *Remember your cane.* But you stay quiet,
like a man contemplating a contained fire,
like a child watching a storm in the distance.

Tremble & Buzz

Another starless Indiana night, another mosquito caught between my shoulder brace and skin: *drink up,* I think, *have one for me, too.* I can't drink. I have a pharmacy on my table, sounds like the cicadas trying to figure out what season it is— but here, it's always nothing, no season, I want to tell them. *Sometimes it's a cold gray. Sometimes warm. But no matter what, eventually the gray wins.* I can feel the mosquito fighting: he didn't know what he was diving into. I take a deep breath to tighten the cuff, end his suffering, though I'll suffer days because of him, a raised itch I can't reach to scratch.

Is grey choking stars out with clouds? The moon haloes enough that I can see the metal glint of my cane, remember some disembodied voice of a well-meaning woman with too much expensive perfume saying, "Did you have a stroke relapse?" I was so shocked I was honest: *I don't know what you mean.* But then I realized. No one knows the stroke might have been the canary, but the coal mine was crashing behind it already. And I don't want to tell her, *you've never heard of this* or *sit down, this will take a while.*

I wish I could hear the cicadas without thinking of how many pills fill my hand in the morning, how many at night. I almost miss the frenzied buzzing of the mosquito. Friends ask how I am, but it's complicated

and I don't want them to think they need to say something profound. I'm glad I don't have to tell them about the constant thrum in my right side, the trembling, the cold, always cold, even burns cold. But at least they didn't hear me earlier when the insurance rep said "things just happen when you get older" and I burst into tears and screamed
I'm 33
I'm 33
I'm 33

But of course, like everything else, that doesn't matter. You can shout into the void, all it does is peel back the layers of your throat until there's blood behind your teeth. I've lost enough blood. And anyway—I can hearing the tiny nose-dive of another angry group of insects, no doubt seeking a blood payment for their friends' death.

If only my blood were payment enough.

Katie Darby Mullins

Elegy for a Crowded Skyline, Formerly Dallas Suburbs

My friend, now divorced, lives
On a Main Street that didn't
Exist when her zip code was mine.
I want to lie in the field

Now decades gone, once more—
Hop the prickled fence to lean
Against solid, stoic cows, staring
At the Methodist church, look

At the playground and remember
Each and every girl I heard
Lost their virginity up against
The hot steel slide covered only in stars.

From there, the ballfields. From there,
The high school I couldn't stand,
Not long enough to stay—I never
Stayed anywhere longer than three years

And schools were no different. Of course—
No grass now. No cows. If I put my head
On the Rowlett asphalt, the gravel, I might
Be able to feel the new buildings sprout,
Growing in the space of my absence.

I can't see the school anymore.
Of course, I didn't want to before,
And it's not about the school.
I want to be sixteen again, see blankness

Spread out in front of me, no decisions
Made, nothing permanent standing
In the way of whatever was going to happen.
I want my cell phone to disappear,

To be completely quiet when the moon
Brightens in a streetlight-free night.
Aggressive signs remind me if I lived there
I'd be home—but this was home,

And now *home* only exists in the geography
Of my brain, the map I created years ago
So I didn't forget the places my feet
Pounded small adventures into before
The city took over the town.

Ritual

In college, I got a tattoo in burnt sienna, *Dayenu,*
Hebrew for 'it was already enough.' The rabbi
taught me that actions create motion, motion
becomes memory, and memory turns to love—
physical ticks, habits, form you, move
like a wind through the universe,
changing the path, forcing you toward love.

Years later as I look at the clock to announce, "It's
8—
get ready, brush teeth, get water." It's so ingrained
it's beyond rehearsed: it's just bedtime. *Become clean,
and let's read.* I watch Grace spin the toothbrush
in her mouth, tickling her tongue with the prickly
bristles:
I can't remember life before this pattern.

She's never clung inside of me: in fact, when I met
Her, she was terrifying, a strange creature of beauty
And need. I don't remember the moment my body
Knew how to love her, instinctively: I don't know
when
My intrigue grew to love. Like a child born back-
wards,
I draw her in to me, now. In ritual, in love.

Voices in Waukesha

The possibility—the endless whispers
of living against all rules, feral
children beholden only to a Shadow—

that's what makes the blade slide in,
not too far beneath her ribs. That's
the ghost-hand driving young hands.

By twelve,
I was old enough to know that life
is a series of ever-narrowing choices,

that each path you choose locks
doors behind you: Slenderman
threw those doors wide, opened

the gates of Hell to this world,
allowed evil thoughts to form
human shapes. Those shapes

climb on top of his tall shoulders,
grasp those hollow bones, and ride,
further away from their promised

destinies and closer to the gaping
maw of disaster. The Internet campfire
gathers, discusses, hushed:

how could this have happened?

But sometimes the blade is easy.
Sometimes we're lured by monsters
we'd die to become.

Neuro, Typical

With Apologies to Robert Frost

You close your eyes to sleep and still you see / The
words and patterns swirling in your head
No black is true when mind directs the scenes—/ A
day, relived, indefinite—"ahead"
Is always planned, but still, rehearsed and lived / Before it's lived: because last winter, you
Can't forget you fell, your brain livid / At your still-
stroke-ridden body, stilled, skewed,
A broken tailbone, students all wide-eyed. / Not now,
you tell yourself: this year, you go
In knowing weakened bones will bend and slide / At
3AM, you plan for the unknown.

> Your eyes are closed, but you
> know you won't sleep.
> You were too close to death.
> You've promises to keep.

Katie Darby Mullins

The King of Rust

I am the king of the rust
and the blanket-curtains
heavy against cracked glass.
I rule the wind, shuffling
mail like cards, spilling
out of unchecked mailboxes

like trash. I let birds float
away from the beer can
windchime. I am the king
of the park across the street,
kids hitting kids, throwing
stones. I watch from stairs

carved in a hill as my subject,
a woman behind the broken window,
fastens the curtains as tight as she can.
Though I know the truth, I pretend
she is a photographer, too much sun
exposing negatives.

I command that the world
stop around me: that the air
hang static, let whirligigs freeze
mid-flight. I order the ants
out of my shoe, the crickets

into silence. But my kingdom
buzzes into a disobedient frenzy:
light flashes against the curtain,
rust on the window pane is matte.
But I am the king. I remember
when the iron was new and strong
and the woman was happy.

I remember before the buildings
burned.

Acknowledgments

I have so many people to thank for making this possible: my parents and sister, who never made me feel like being a poet was anything other than a great choice; my Underwater Sunshine Family; my students (especially Charlie Ericson, Natalie Christy, AJ Dick, Justin Sczesny, Morgan Severeid, and Krys Wininger: you know what you did); my 'fake parents,' Rob and Tiffany; and my mentors, starting with the English department at Garland High School and the professors at UE, Pinckney Benedict, and the writers at Spalding University.

A special thanks to Kaveh Akbar and Paige Lewis for giving me an incredible 'first book' story.

I also wouldn't be here without the Neuro ICU team at Deaconess Hospital in Evansville, Indiana, especially Dr. Jason Meckler and my nurse, Teresa Cummings; or without my ride-or-die Dr. Roy Arnold and my PT, Dr. Ryan Wood.

A special thanks to Brooks, who is so much more important to me than a publisher: his friendship has spanned a decade and I still look forward to seeing his smile on editorial calls.

I'd also like to thank Corinna Schroeder, who has been both a friend and an idol to me, Eryn Yetts-Teeling, who never gave up on my miraculous turnaround, and Charlie, who kept a close eye on me at work when I went back.

I also always promised myself I'd put this in my first book, but a special thanks to my pal Adam, who once told me the secret to singing—and writing—was learning to love your own voice.

But none of this would have been possible without my husband, Andy, who has been doggedly excited about my writing even when I haven't been, and my kid, Grace, who makes every day a good one just by virtue of being on the planet.

Attributions

"Why Male Birds Have Such Bright Feathers" was originally printed in the *Santa Ana Review*

"Animal Stress" was originally printed in *Waterhouse Review*

"What I Think Of When You Say You Aren't Afraid of Anything" was originally published in *Big Lucks*

"Ritual" was originally printed in the *Ottawa Arts Review*

"Voices in Waukesha" was originally printed in *The San Diego Reader*

"King of Rust" was originally published in *Cider Press Review*

About the Author:

Katie Darby Mullins teaches creative writing at the University of Evansville. In addition to being nominated for both the Pushcart Prize and Best of the Net multiple times, she's been published or has work forthcoming in journals like *Barrelhouse*, *The Rumpus*, *Iron Horse*, *Hobart*, *Hawaii Pacific Review*, *BOAAT Press*, *Harpur Palate*, *Prime Number*, *Big Lucks*, and *Pithead Chapel*. She helped found and is the  executive writer for the Underwater Sunshine Fest, a NYC-based music festival for indie rock bands. Interact with her via Twitter at @katieUWSF.

About the Publisher:

Summer Camp Publishing is an independent press specializing in brief works of large ambition. For author and press correspondence, classroom copies, speaking engagement inquires and information about existing and upcoming publications, please visit us online at http://www.summercampbooks.com.

CPSIA information can be obtained
at www.ICGtesting.com
Printed in the USA
LVHW092045210221
679522LV00007B/621